W9-AHG-861

BOOK MARKS

If you wish to keep a record
that you have read this book,
you may use the space
provided to mark a private
code. Please do not mark the
book in any other way.

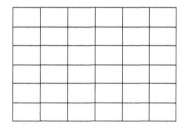

Meet the
SUPREME
COURT

By Drew Nelson

Gareth Stevens
Publishing

Please visit our website, www.garethstevens.com. For a free color catalog of all our high-quality books, call toll free 1-800-542-2595 or fax 1-877-542-2596.

Library of Congress Cataloging-in-Publication Data

Nelson, Drew, 1986-
Meet the Supreme Court / Drew Nelson.
    p. cm. — (A guide to your government)
Includes index.
ISBN 978-1-4339-7269-0 (pbk.)
ISBN 978-1-4339-7270-6 (6-pack)
ISBN 978-1-4339-7268-3 (library binding)
1. United States. Supreme Court—Juvenile literature. I. Title.
KF8742.N45 2012
347.73'26—dc23

2012006952

First Edition

Published in 2013 by
Gareth Stevens Publishing
111 East 14th Street, Suite 349
New York, NY 10003

Copyright © 2013 Gareth Stevens Publishing

Designer: Daniel Hosek
Editor: Kristen Rajczak

Photo credits: Cover, pp. 1, 23 (inset) Mark Wilson/Getty Images; p. 5 (main image) MPI/Getty Images; p. 5 (Constitution) Fotosearch/Getty Images; p. 7 Gary Blakeley/Shutterstock.com; p. 9 Stock Montage/Getty Images; p. 11 (Dred Scott) Photo Researchers/Getty Images; p. 11 (Roger Taney) Hulton Archive/Getty Images; p. 13 Kean Collection/Getty Images; p. 15 Harris & Ewing/Buyenlarge/Getty Images; p. 17 Trascendental Graphics/Getty Images; p. 19 Carl Iwasaki/Time & Life Pictures/Getty Images; pp. 21, 23 (main image), 27 Alex Wong/Getty Images; p. 25 Mandel Ngan/AFP/Getty Images; p. 28 Bachrach/Getty Images; p. 29 Chip Somodevilla/Getty Images.

Printed in the United States of America

CPSIA compliance information: Batch #CS12GS: For further information contact Gareth Stevens, New York, New York at 1-800-542-2595.

CONTENTS

Words in the glossary appear in **bold** type
the first time they are used in the text.

THE EARLY US GOVERNMENT

Following the **American Revolution**, the young United States needed a new government. They had been colonies under the rule of the British king, so the Founding Fathers didn't want another single powerful ruler. The first plan for a US government was the Articles of Confederation. Under the Articles, the federal government was weak and couldn't collect taxes to fund its work or form an army.

The country's leaders met in 1787 to write a new set of rules for the government. This document, the US Constitution, created three branches of government and divided duties between them. It also provided a system of checks and balances for each branch to keep an eye on the others' powers.

FEDERAL *Fact*
Under the Articles of Confederation, there wasn't a national court system.

4

We the People

The US Constitution is the piece of writing that outlines the nation's laws and gives power to the federal government. It was written by representatives from each state at the Constitutional Convention in Philadelphia, Pennsylvania. These men signed it on September 17, 1787. Then, each state had to decide whether it wanted to approve the new plan for government. By 1789, two-thirds of the states had voted in favor of the Constitution, and the new government began working.

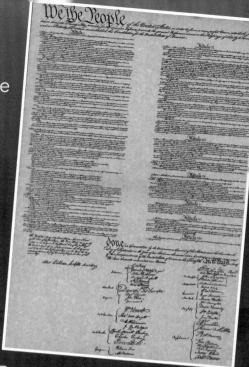

The Founding Fathers knew it was important to include a court system in the government created by the US Constitution.

THE JUDICIAL BRANCH

The federal government is split into three branches: the executive branch, the legislative branch, and the judicial branch. The executive branch is the president, vice president, the president's cabinet, and various departments and agencies. The legislative branch is Congress, made up of the Senate and the House of Representatives. The judicial branch is the Supreme Court and the federal courts under it.

The Supreme Court often checks up on the other two branches of government. Many of the cases it hears review laws made by Congress and the actions of the president and other government officials. The Supreme Court's job is to determine if a law or an act is constitutional, which means that it follows the laws in the Constitution. If parts of a law or someone's actions are ruled unconstitutional, they're stopped.

FEDERAL *Fact*

The legislative branch has a very powerful check over the Supreme Court. It can **impeach** justices as well as approve their appointments.

The US Supreme Court makes its decisions in this beautiful building located in Washington, DC.

Checks on the Judicial Branch

The executive and legislative branches check the Supreme Court, too. The president is the only one who can appoint justices to the Supreme Court. Congress approves these choices, which gives it a chance to check the powers of both the judicial and executive branches. The president can also give pardons, which means he can stop or lessen the punishments of people or organizations that the court system has found guilty.

THE FIRST COURT

Even though the Constitution created the Supreme Court, it was left up to Congress to decide what the makeup of the court would be. With the Judiciary Act of 1789, Congress set up a court with six justices that would deal with cases that involved states, ambassadors, or treaties. Many of the cases that the first Supreme Court justices heard were actually between individual states and the United States itself!

The act also broke the nation into districts and assigned one judge and court to each. Then, circuit courts were created to serve as a higher court to several districts. Two Supreme Court justices sat in each of the three circuits a few times a year.

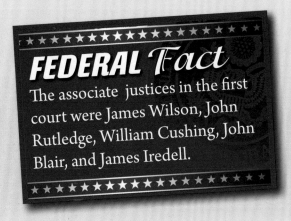

FEDERAL *Fact*

The associate justices in the first court were James Wilson, John Rutledge, William Cushing, John Blair, and James Iredell.

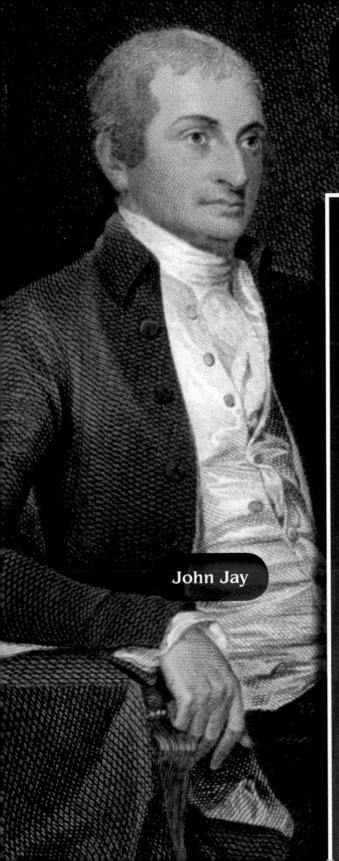

John Jay

The Justices of the First Court

The six justices who made up the first Supreme Court had a tough job. Since no one had done it before, they had to figure out what their powers were and how to do what they needed to in court. The first chief justice of the Supreme Court was John Jay. He held the position from 1789 to 1795. Chief Justice Jay was used to having important jobs, though. He was one of the men who signed the treaty with England after the American Revolution.

COURT EXPANSION

Over the next 20 years, the population of the United States grew quickly, especially in new states like Kentucky, Tennessee, and Ohio. In 1807, Congress voted to increase the size of the Supreme Court from six to seven justices. This allowed the court to better handle the concerns of a higher population and the increased number of cases it was seeing.

Congress changed the number of justices several times during the 1800s. In 1837, the number of justices was increased to nine, and during the **American Civil War** in the 1860s, the number rose to 10. After the Civil War ended, the number of justices was lowered to eight. Then, in 1869, it was raised back to nine, which is the size it has been since then.

FEDERAL *Fact*

During the first 70 years of the court, there were only five chief justices.

Circuit Expansion

As the number of justices on the Supreme Court changed, so did the number of different circuit courts. Originally, there were only three circuits within the 13 states of the United States. By 1860, there were already 10 different circuits to match the growing population and geographic area of the United States, including one for California and Oregon. When the justices had to travel to hear cases at the various circuit courts, they called it "riding the circuit."

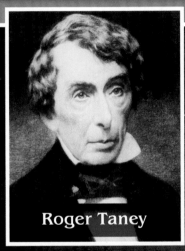

Roger Taney

In 1857, Chief Justice Roger Taney led the Supreme Court in its ruling of a case brought by a black man named Dred Scott. The decision said that blacks, whether slaves or free, weren't American citizens and didn't have the right to bring a case to court.

Dred Scott

11

AFTER THE CIVIL WAR

Things changed in the Supreme Court after the Civil War. The Judiciary Act of 1869 permanently set the number of justices in the Supreme Court at nine and made it so they only had to work in the circuit courts once every 2 years. This way, they could spend more time working on cases that came to the Supreme Court.

The number of cases that were brought to the Supreme Court rose quickly during the late 1800s. From 1860 to 1890, the number of cases heard each term increased from 310 to 1,816. Because of this, in 1891, Congress passed a law stating that Supreme Court justices didn't have to work in the circuit courts at all, and they could focus entirely on Supreme Court cases.

FEDERAL Fact

The Judiciary Act of 1869 changed the rules on how long justices had to serve. According to this law, if they serve for 10 years and are at least 70 years old, they can retire and still receive full pay.

John S. Rock was the first black person allowed to argue a case before the Supreme Court—and he did so in 1865, only 8 years after Dred Scott was kept out.

Issues After the Civil War

There were two main reasons for the increase in cases the Supreme Court heard after the Civil War. The first was the continuing increase in population. The second was that the court had to **preside** over many cases having to do with the end of slavery in the South. There were more than 4 million freed slaves who were now finding a place in American society, and it was the Supreme Court's job to protect them under the Constitution.

THE RISE OF BIG BUSINESS

From the late 1800s to the 1920s, many of the cases the Supreme Court presided over had to do with business. The **Industrial Revolution** was moving people to cities and making life difficult for farmers. Corporations and businessmen were becoming more powerful, while conditions were getting worse for the people who worked for them.

Several of the cases heard by the Supreme Court concerned **monopolies**, the federal regulation of growing businesses, and the conditions in which people were working. Many also had to do with new immigration laws, as many immigrants came to the United States during this time. Immigrants are people who move to the United States from other countries. Just like the freed slaves, they needed the Supreme Court to protect their constitutional rights as new citizens.

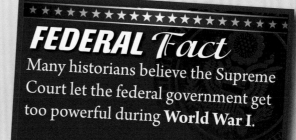

FEDERAL *Fact*

Many historians believe the Supreme Court let the federal government get too powerful during **World War I**.

The Supreme Court During War

The United States became involved in World War I in 1917. The federal government had to become much more powerful to win the war, and many bills were passed controlling the country's economy, manufacturing, military draft, and spending. It was the Supreme Court's job to hear cases brought before it regarding the constitutionality of government actions during this time.

Five constitutional amendments passed between 1869 and 1920, one awarding women the right to vote. The Supreme Court now had even more law to interpret.

CRASH AND WAR

The three decades following World War I were a busy time for the Supreme Court. In the early 1930s, the United States faced the Great Depression, the worst economic **crisis** in its history. One out of every four people didn't have a job, and many people lost their homes and life savings. The president and Congress tried to regulate the economy. At first, the Supreme Court disagreed with many of their plans and judged them to be unconstitutional. After the president proposed a plan to add more justices to the court, however, the Supreme Court started to allow these laws.

Many historians believe **World War II** pulled the United States out of the Great Depression. The Supreme Court allowed the executive branch to again assume greater wartime powers and declare war in 1941.

FEDERAL Fact
President Franklin D. Roosevelt tried to "pack the court" with more justices because he worried the Supreme Court would rule some of the biggest parts of his economic plan, called the New Deal, unconstitutional.

Many people, such as those waiting in line for bread here, relied on new government programs for help during the Great Depression.

Change in the Court

One major reason the Supreme Court seemed to change its position and help the president during the Great Depression and World War II was that many justices left the court in the 1930s. Between 1937 and 1939, three justices retired from the court and two justices died. President Roosevelt used his power to appoint justices and filled those five spots with people who supported him. After that, he had more than half of the justices on his side.

RIGHTS FOR ALL

Since World War II, the biggest focus of the Supreme Court has been protecting the rights of American citizens. During the 1960s, many important civil rights cases having to do with equality for African Americans came before the court. With its help, black Americans gained many rights, such as the right to go to the same schools as white students and the right to have the same jobs as everyone else.

Over the next 40 years, the Supreme Court helped many other groups of American citizens in their search for equality. The court looked at many laws and overturned those that prevented citizens from receiving their full rights. Women, young people, the disabled, and gay people have all been helped by Supreme Court rulings about civil rights.

FEDERAL *Fact*

The Supreme Court ruled in *Brown v. Board of Education* (1954) that segregation in schools violated the Fourteenth Amendment of the Constitution, which guarantees equal protection under the law for all and forbids states from making laws that limit citizens' privileges.

This picture shows students and parents who were represented by Brown v. Board of Education.

School Segregation

One of the most famous Supreme Court cases from the civil rights era is *Brown v. Board of Education* (1954). It dealt with laws that prevented black students from attending the same schools as white students. Keeping facilities separate for different races is called segregation. The Supreme Court found these laws unconstitutional and stated that the government couldn't separate people for public schooling based only on race. This led to more cases that challenged segregation in other areas of American life.

19

SUPREME STRUCTURE

The current Supreme Court is made up of one chief justice and eight associate justices. Their term begins on the first Monday in October, and they usually hear cases until late June or early July of the next year. Over the course of the term, the justices have different kinds of sessions that last for about 2 weeks at a time. During sessions called sittings, justices hear cases and deliver opinions. During the recesses, they work on the business of the court, studying upcoming cases and writing their opinions.

There can be up to 24 cases argued during each sitting. Usually, each side in a case gets 30 minutes to argue its point. Because most of the cases involve reviewing decisions from other cases, there are no juries and no witnesses, just representatives of the two sides and the justices.

FEDERAL Fact

As of 2012, there have been 112 different justices in the Supreme Court. The average amount of time each justice has served is 16 years.

Working at the Court

Even though the nine justices are the only people involved in the decision of a case, there are many more people who work for the Supreme Court to make everything run smoothly. Other people who work in the Supreme Court include the counselor to the chief justice, the clerk, the librarian, the marshal, the reporter of decisions, the court counsel, the curator, the director of information technology, and the public information officer.

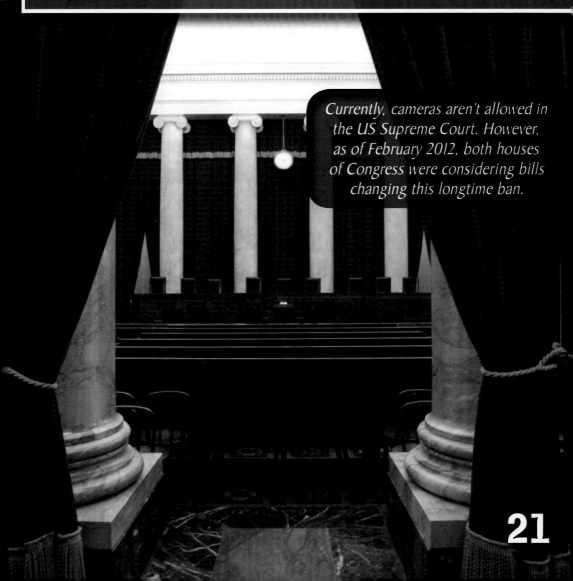

Currently, cameras aren't allowed in the US Supreme Court. However, as of February 2012, both houses of Congress were considering bills changing this longtime ban.

THE APPOINTMENT PROCESS

The president nominates justices to the Supreme Court when there's an open seat, but the appointment process isn't as easy as it seems. Usually, the White House counsel, the **attorney general**, and lawyers from the Justice Department put together a list of possible nominees and interview them. Then they present that list to the president. The president chooses a nominee based on their qualifications, political views, and the likelihood they'll be approved by the Senate.

After that, the 100 members of the Senate vote on whether the president's selection should be on the Supreme Court. Before the vote, the nominee is brought before the Senate Judiciary Committee and asked questions about their legal record and political beliefs. If the Senate is satisfied with the nominee's answers, the individual is approved. Since 1789, the Senate has only rejected the president's nominee 12 times.

FEDERAL *Fact*

The youngest justice of the Supreme Court was Joseph Story. He was 32 years old when he took office in 1811.

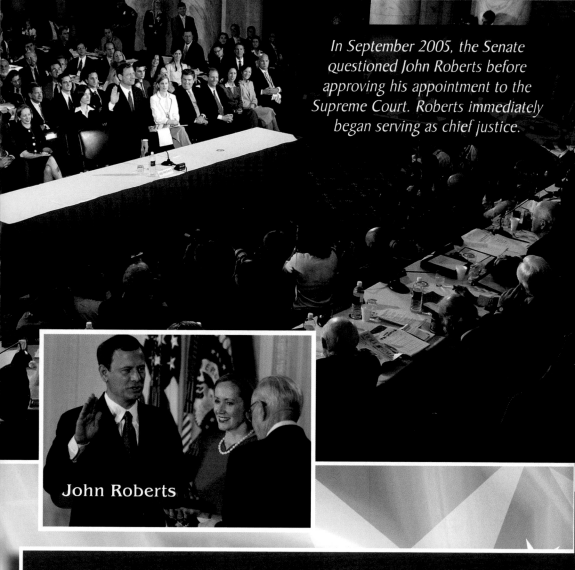

In September 2005, the Senate questioned John Roberts before approving his appointment to the Supreme Court. Roberts immediately began serving as chief justice.

John Roberts

How to Become a Justice

The Constitution sets no requirements for Supreme Court appointees. However, there are a few things that make an appointment more likely. First, be a graduate from the law school at Harvard University or Yale University. Of the nine justices on the Supreme Court in 2012, five graduated from Harvard, and three graduated from Yale. Second, be born in the United States. Only six people born outside the United States have ever been appointed justices.

23

JUDICIAL REVIEW AND WRITS

The Supreme Court's most important power is judicial review. This is the court's ability to hear cases assessing government actions and decide if these actions are constitutional. Today, judicial review is the main power the Supreme Court exercises. It isn't in the Constitution, though. The court gave itself this power in 1803 in the court case *Marbury v. Madison.*

The Supreme Court also has the power to issue court orders called writs. A writ of habeas corpus allows people who have been arrested, imprisoned, or convicted to see if their **judicial process** was constitutional. A writ of mandamus orders a government official to do something required by their job, and a writ of prohibition stops them from doing something not allowed by their job.

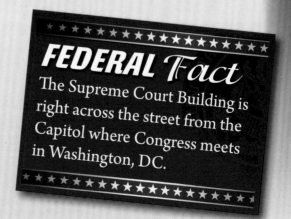

FEDERAL Fact

The Supreme Court Building is right across the street from the Capitol where Congress meets in Washington, DC.

It's common for people to protest outside the Supreme Court, especially when a case concerning a big political issue is being heard.

Home of the Supreme Court

Even though the Supreme Court was created in 1789, it didn't have a building of its own until 1935. Before that, the court met in New York City; Philadelphia, Pennsylvania; and then a few different locations in Washington, DC. For a long time, the Supreme Court used part of the Capitol building that wasn't being used by Congress. At one point, the Supreme Court actually met in a private house!

LANDMARK CASES

★ ★ ★ ★ ★ ★ ★ ★ ★ ★ ★ ★ ★ ★ ★ ★ ★

The Supreme Court has heard many cases during the more than 200 years it's been around, but a few cases stand out as especially important. Some of these decisions affect our lives every day, while others only affect the government.

In *McCulloch v. Maryland* (1819), the Supreme Court established Congress's ability to pass laws "necessary and proper" to the running of the nation.

The court decided in *Miranda v. Arizona* (1966) that Ernesto Miranda's confession to a crime had to be thrown out because the police failed to inform him of some of his rights. Today, when someone is arrested, police recite a list of rights called "Miranda rights."

In *Tinker v. Des Moines* (1969), the court determined that students still have the right to freedom of speech and expression while they are on school grounds.

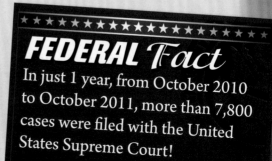

FEDERAL *Fact*

In just 1 year, from October 2010 to October 2011, more than 7,800 cases were filed with the United States Supreme Court!

In 2000, a Supreme Court case decided the presidential election! Supporters of both sides stood outside the court while the case was argued.

Supreme Traditions

The Supreme Court follows many traditions, some of which have been around since the first days of the court. The justices always sit with the chief justice in the center. The justice who has been on the court the longest sits to the chief justice's right, and the one who has served second longest sits to the left. The justices have worn black robes in court since 1800 and have all shaken hands with each other before sitting down since the late 1800s.

RECENT JUSTICES

There's been a lot of turnover in the Supreme Court in recent years. Since 2005, four new justices have taken seats in the court.

In September 2005, John Roberts became the newest chief justice. President George W. Bush nominated him. In January 2006, Samuel Alito took the court seat of retiring justice Sandra Day O'Connor. Justice O'Connor was the first woman to serve on the Supreme Court.

In August 2009, Sonia Sotomayor became the first Supreme Court justice of Hispanic descent when she replaced Justice David Souter. She was appointed by President Barack Obama. Elena Kagan became a Supreme Court justice in August 2010 after working as the head of Harvard Law School.

FEDERAL *Fact*
The oldest person to serve as a Supreme Court justice was Oliver Wendell Holmes Jr. He was 90 years old when he retired in 1932.

Sonia Sotomayor was approved by the Senate as the third woman to ever serve as a justice on the Supreme Court.

The Long and Short of It

Once justices are appointed to the Supreme Court, they can keep the position for as long as they want. The justice who served on the court for the longest time was William O. Douglas. He was a Supreme Court justice for 36 years, 7 months, and 8 days. The justice who served the shortest term was Thomas Johnson. He only

GLOSSARY

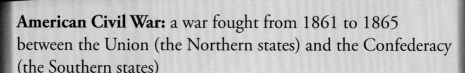

American Civil War: a war fought from 1861 to 1865 between the Union (the Northern states) and the Confederacy (the Southern states)

American Revolution: the war in which the colonies won their freedom from England (1775–1783)

attorney general: the chief law officer of the United States. The attorney general heads the US Department of Justice.

crisis: a situation in which events are very difficult or uncertain and action must be taken to avoid disaster

impeach: to charge a government official with wrongdoing while in office

Industrial Revolution: the period during the late 18th and early 19th centuries when many countries moved from a farming-based economy to one based on business and manufacturing

judicial process: the rights given to someone accused of a crime

monopoly: the complete control by one person or company over certain goods or services

preside: to be in charge

World War I: the global conflict from 1914 to 1918 in which the United States joined with England, France, Russia, Italy, and Japan

World War II: the global conflict from 1939 to 1945 in which the United States joined with the Allied nations, including France, England, and the Soviet Union

30

FOR MORE INFORMATION

Books

DiPrimio, Pete. *The Judicial Branch*. Hockessin, DE: M. Lane, 2012.

Eccleston, Linda M. *When I Grow Up, I Want to Be a Supreme Court Justice: A Young Person's Guide to Understanding the United States Federal Judiciary*. Scotts Valley, CA: CreateSpace, 2011.

Websites

Judicial Branch: The Supreme Court
www.congressforkids.net/Judicialbranch_supremecourt.htm
Read more about the Supreme Court and justices.

The Supreme Court Historical Society
www.supremecourthistory.org
Read more about the history of the Supreme Court and listen to important court arguments and decisions.

Supreme Court of the United States
www.supremecourt.gov
Keep up to date about the latest news and cases being heard at the Supreme Court.

INDEX

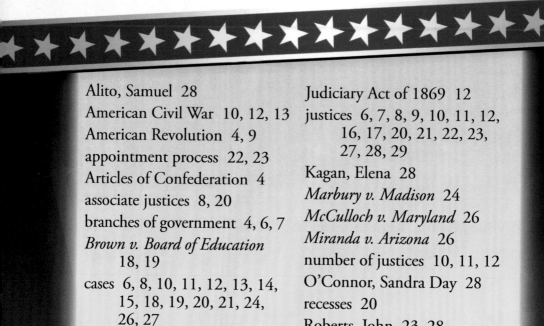